Chomp! Munch! Chew!

KAREN WALLACE & ROSS COLLINS

W
FRANKLIN WATTS
NEW YORK • LONDON • SYDNEY

All animals need food to live. From an anteater to a seal, every animal eats its food in its own special way.

GULP!

CHEW!

SLURP!

MUNCH!

SNAP!

nibble
nibble
nibble

3

Grass grows almost everywhere –
so it's easy to find.

A cow pulls up grass.

CHOMP! CHOMP! CHOMP!

She chews it with her back teeth.

Snails SCRAPE grass with tiny rows of teeth.

All sorts of animals eat grass, and they all have different ways of eating it.

Hold it! Slice it! This prairie dog's long front teeth are just right for the job.

MUNCH! MUNCH! MUNCH!

Some animals eat plants, bushes and trees.
They chew and suck on the flowers and leaves.
They scrape the bark and dig up the roots.

High thorny twigs are a giraffe's favourite food.

6

This dik-dik is no bigger than a hare.

He likes to NIBBLE bushes near the ground.

GRUNT! GRUNT! GRUNT! GRUNT!

Warthogs dig up roots and bulbs with their snouts.

There are plenty of plants growing underwater, too!

A water hyacinth tastes great to a manatee!

Grass carp prefer to GRAZE on water weed.

9

Where would animals be without TEETH?
Some even grow new ones when their old
ones wear out!

Ever met a shark
with saw-tooth teeth?
A blue shark
CHOMPS
anything from
sardines to squid.

Monitor lizards are scavengers. They need strong teeth to RIP and TEAR flesh.

A gharial's teeth are as sharp as needles. And there are always enough to GRAB a slippery fish.

11

Some animals don't have teeth at all.
They sieve their food.

Shoveler ducks have bills like shovels. They strain
the water for snails and little animals.

A flamingo
swings his beak
from side
to side
to get his food.

A manta ray **SUCKS** in gallons of water to trap thousands of tiny creatures in his mouth.

Jaws, claws or a powerful beak
can crack open a tasty snack!

A crab's claws can snap
your finger! This limpet's
shell is easy to break.

14

How does a parrot open a nut? He GRIPS and CRACKS.

A Staffordshire bull~terrier has specially strong jaws. Don't worry! He's happy GNAWING a bone.

Some animals spit to catch their food.

ZAP! A spitting cobra dims poison at his victim's eyes.

Flies spit on their food to make it soft and watery. Then they SUCK it up! ugh!

SPLAT!

An archer fish rarely misses!

Some animals swallow their food whole.

When there are fish to be had dolphins eat them head first.

Open **WIDE !**

This snake is having an egg for breakfast.

When a pelican swallows a fish, there's always room for more.

Birds, small mammals and insects
suck and lick nectar from flowers!

A hawkmoth has a special tube that's three times longer than he is!

A pygmy possum LAPS nectar,
and spreads pollen
from blossom to blossom.

This hummingbird can reach the bottom of his favourite flower.

Some animals kill their food
with a poisonous sting or a bite.

A jellyfish has long stinging tentacles. Each one can kill a tiny fish.

When a Scorpion looks like this WATCH OUT! He is ready to STRIKE!

Centipedes have poisonous fangs. Can you see where they are?

23

Koalas and giant pandas only eat one kind of food each.

CHOMP! CHOMP!

A koala eats eucalyptus leaves. He PUNCHES through them with a razor sharp tooth.

A giant panda eats bamboo. He MUNCHES and CRUNCHES for almost twelve hours a day!

25

Some animals use tools to help them eat their food. Others just throw it on the ground!

Chimpanzees use a stick to catch termites. Then they **LICK** them off!

A sea otter **SMASHES** a clam against a flat stone.

There's only one way for a bird to **CRUSH** a mussel.

Seagulls know exactly what to do!

27

All animals need food to live. People do, too!

And just like other animals, we eat it in lots of different ways!

29

Further information

Anteater – A long tongue, toothless jaws and a tiny mouth make it possible for an anteater to suck up its favourite food – ants (see page 2).

Dolphin – Dolphins always eat fish head first so that the fish's scales stay flat when it is swallowed (see page 18).

Anteater

Giant panda
A panda's thumb is very long so that it can easily grip the bamboo shoots it likes to eat (see pages 24, 25).

Domestic cat

Giraffe – A giraffe has thick, fleshy lips that protect its mouth from sharp, spiky thorns (see page 6).

Parrot – Once parrots have cracked open a nut, they use their thick, strong tongue to lick out the kernel (see page 14).

Manatee

Puffin

Pelican – Pelicans fish in horseshoe-shaped groups to herd their prey together and make the fish easier to catch (see page 19).

Pelican

Scavenger – A scavenger, such as a monitor lizard, eats any dead meat it can find, including animals killed by other animals (see page 11).

Shark – Sharks' teeth are curved backwards so that, once caught, their prey cannot escape (see page 10).

For Connie Ramsay – KW
For manic Alex – RC

This edition 2014

First published by Franklin Watts,
338 Euston Road, London NW1 3BH

Franklin Watts Australia,
Level 17 / 207 Kent Street, Sydney NSW 2000

Text © 1999 Karen Wallace
Illustrations © 1999 Ross Collins
Notes and activities © 2004, 2014 Franklin Watts

Series editor: Rachel Cooke
Art director: Robert Walster
Consultant: Dr Jim Flegg

A CIP catalogue record is available from the British Library.
Dewey Classification 574

Printed in China

ISBN 978 1 4451 2887 0

Franklin Watts is a division of Hachette Children's Books,
an Hachette UK company. www.hachette.co.uk